Write A Book Faster Today

Writing Habits That Destroy Writer's Block

Emma Fisher

Copyright © 2017 Pinnacle Publishers, LLC

All rights reserved.

ISBN: 1546825762
ISBN-13: 978-1546825760

This document is geared towards providing exact and reliable information in regards to the topic and issue covered. The publication is sold with the idea that the publisher is not required to render accounting, officially permitted, or otherwise, qualified services. If advice is necessary, legal or professional, a practiced individual in the profession should be ordered.
- From a Declaration of Principles which was accepted and approved equally by a Committee of the American Bar Association and a Committee of Publishers and Associations.
In no way is it legal to reproduce, duplicate, or transmit any part of this document in either electronic means or in printed format. Recording of this publication is strictly prohibited and any storage of this document is not allowed unless with written permission from the publisher. All rights reserved.
The information provided herein is stated to be truthful and consistent, in that any liability, in terms of inattention or otherwise, by any usage or abuse of any policies, processes, or directions contained within is the solitary and utter responsibility of the recipient reader. Under no circumstances will any legal responsibility or blame be held against the publisher for any reparation, damages, or monetary loss due to the information herein, either directly or indirectly.
Respective authors own all copyrights not held by the publisher.
The information herein is offered for informational purposes solely, and is universal as so. The presentation of the information is without contract or any type of guarantee assurance.
The trademarks that are used are without any consent, and the publication of the trademark is without permission or backing by the trademark owner. All trademarks and brands within this book are for clarifying purposes only and are the owned by the owners themselves, not affiliated with this document.

CONTENTS

	Introduction	v
1	Are You a Writer?	1
2	The Journey Begins	5
3	The Blank Page	9
4	Writing Flow in the Thick of It	16
5	It's Done, Now What	22
6	Good Habits to Remember	26
	Conclusion	31

INTRODUCTION

Writer's block is not a diagnosed condition you'll find in any medical journal, but for many writers out there, it can feel like a real condition that can seem incurable. At its most basic, writer's block is defined as a period when a writer finds themselves unable to proceed with their writing whether from lack of ideas or issues in how to get those ideas onto the paper successfully.

It happens to many writers, more than you might expect. Successful writers like JK Rowling and George RR Martin have both expressed moments where writer's block slowed down their process. It's not uncommon and it doesn't make you a bad writer. But how you react to it and what you do to tackle it will set apart the true writers from those just dabbling with a hobby.

So, how do you tackle it? How do you learn to write faster? How do you get that writer flow and get yourself able to keep it going across multiple writing sessions? This book is going to provide you with answers, but at the end of the day, it's up to you to see through your writing and get into good habits. This is a place to start, but it ends with your drive.

Are you ready to make yourself the best writer you can be?

THANK YOU FOR BUYING THIS PINNACLE PUBLISHERS BOOK!

Join our mailing list and get updates on new releases, deals, bonus content and other great books from Pinnacle Publishers. We also give away a new eBook every week completely free!

Scan the Above QR Code to Sign Up

Or visit us online to sign up at
www.pinnaclepublish.com/newsletter

CHAPTER 1: ARE YOU A WRITER?

The legendary Margaret Atwood, the author of more than 40 books, and often considered the grandmother of the modern dystopian novel had a very simple answer when asked by an audience member at a signing of The Handmaid's Tale at a Toronto bookstore what advice she had for young writers: "Are you writing? If you say yes then congratulations, you're a writer. If you say no, then you're not a writer. But you're thinking about it." Likewise, Stephen King often says the key to cultivating writing and writing habits is to get in the habit of producing at least 2,000 words a day.

Unfortunately, there is no secret to becoming a successful writer. There is no quick trick, no guru or oracle to converse with that will deliver you to all the riches and recognition you've wanted for your writing. It comes down to simply sitting at the desk and getting words onto the page. And, unfortunately, Margaret Atwood also pointed out that it's never going to get easier. "You're always starting from a blank page," she said. Whether you're a 20-year-old college student or a tried citizen on your way to retirement. The great equalizer among writers isn't death, it's the first word on the blank page.

Let's say you answered that question in the negative, no, you're not writing. By Margaret Atwood's definition, you're not a writer, but you're thinking about it. The second part of that statement is really what's important here. You're not a writer, but you want to be. Sometimes, though, it's not all that easy to make it happen. There are other ways to tell if you're destined for the written word or just dabbling in an idea.

Chuck Wendig, one of the most prolific genre writers out there, has a nifty blog post on his website that tackles the question of writer identity on a more nuanced level. He lists off some points that could suggest you might be a writer in the making, even if you're not quite there yet. And that's an excellent and encouraging place to start for anyone who has found themselves victimized by writer's block and the fear of the blank page:

- **Proofreading everything**. By this, Wendig doesn't necessarily mean sitting there with a red pen and marking off mistakes. But you're out at dinner and have comments about the menu, or maybe a street advertisement is missing a comma. You notice these things. They bother you. And it goes farther than that, you critique movies based on the screenplay structure, much to the ire of your friends, you were that kid in English class saying you didn't like *Hamlet* because you would have taken the story in a different direction.

- **Imaginary friends**. For this, Wendig is specifically talking about imaginary friends. You may have had yourself an imaginary friend to talk to or an entire cabal of characters following you around. This is the beginning of creativity, the burst of imagination from a young age. It doesn't necessarily manifest just in the form of imaginary friends, maybe you made up secret worlds, played games with characters from shows or movies that weren't actually there. Writing has a lot to do with playing. After all, Albert Einstein once said: "Creativity is intelligence having fun."

- **Conversations with no one**. This is possibly one of the most neurotic things writers are known to do. Whether you're testing out dialogue by mumbling out conversations or having full-blown conversations with your characters yourself. It's a common tactic, one we'll get to later in the book, to generate conversations between yourself and characters to get to know them. You take them out for coffee, ask them their thoughts on a movie, want to know how their night went. And it all makes perfect sense to you.

- **Pens and notebooks everywhere**. I know for myself, I have a problem of continually buying notebooks. I fill them up quick with scribbles and notes and need to move onto the next one. I steal pens often, whether or not they've got the name of some sex store stamped on the side or not. These are the tools of the trade, and you can't get enough of them. You collect these things and you never want to get rid of them. You've got a whole box of filled notebooks and used pens under your bed.

- **You don't get along well with 'non-readers'**. There is a famous quote from John Waters: "If you go home with somebody and they don't have books, don't fuck them." For a writer, this is a religious commandment. People who don't read, who don't own more than one or two books, they're not the person for you. They operate on a different frequency, in a different world. And you want nothing to do with it.

- **Your brain is constantly on inspiration mode**. Wendig describes the writer's brain as an intrusive spam email barrage of constant inspiration. You could be sitting in the doctor's office, you could be grocery shopping, you could be just about to fall asleep and bam, a story strikes you. You've somehow found yourself subscribed to a constant stream of ideas that you just can't seem to shut off.

- **You often know how to do it differently**. This goes along with the proofreading point at the top, but writers are often well aware of how they might change a movie or a book or a TV show to tighten it up.

There are some other, more comic check marks at the end of Wendig's list (such as affinity for whiskey or a desire to find a spouse with health insurance) but the important ones are there. Those bullet points are the elements of a writer's mind. If a few of these seem to describe you, or maybe all of them, then congrats, you've conquered your first step to realizing your writerly potential.

But what do you do with this knowledge? How do you more forward to embrace your destiny? How do you get the barrage of ideas or the need to constantly edit under control long enough to form a coherent story or paper or whatever it is you find yourself writing? The answer is a simple one but much easier said than done:

Discipline.

This book is going to be all about discipline, in one way or another. It's going to be discussed as many things: maybe writing prompts or goals, but at the end of the day writing is all about discipline. A lot of people don't like to hear this. Making art is hard. And getting over the mental blocks and forcing yourself to do something can be incredibly stressful and anxiety inducing.

But there are ways to take it on. The following chapters are going to outline ways you can keep yourself writing, even when it seems you're at the end of your rope or just don't want anything to do with the work you're creating any more. The biggest thing to remember is that these feelings are felt by every writer at some point. The difference is, those that are successful are those that can overcome the blocks in their own head. The fact of the matter is, your greatest adversary and your greatest enemy is going to be yourself.

So, if you're ready to take on that person in the mirror, let's begin the journey of how to demolish writer's block, how to get that workflow flowing, and how to get those word counts up.

CHAPTER 2: THE JOURNEY BEGINS

Before we jump completely into the practices for discipline as a writer, there are some things you'll want to cover for yourself: your own backstory as the main character in the great and epic tale of your life. You know you're a writer, in your heart. But how do you get other people to know? It's not unlike King Arthur. The sword (or in this case, the proverbial pen) has chosen you, plucked you from nothing, but you still have a long way to go before you can become king (a writer). So, where do you begin? Who is your Merlin? Where do you find guidance?

There's plenty of ways to become a writer and different paths can lead to different writer types across different markets. The writer's voice, that thing that makes them stand out from a sea of people shouting into the ether, is born in how and where your education as a writer begins.

Think of it like being a Jedi. Maybe you're trained in the old Jedi Order, with master's a strict protocol. Maybe you're like Luke and have to learn what you can from masters of a bygone era with no funded resources or organization at your back. Maybe you're like Rey and find yourself plucked out of obscurity and told this is a destiny you need to pursue.

There's plenty of ways you could find yourself on a path to writerhood and while none of them are better than the other, objectively, they will guide you to different spots in life and different outcomes.

Option 1: The Trained Padawan

This is the path that most often produces the literary type of writer. Though many writers across all genres went to school and got themselves a degree in writing, this path almost exclusively produces the high literary types who submit work to Writer's Digest regularly and have won a bunch of prestigious medals before they even graduate.

For the creative writer, this is the path that will lead you to the works of Ernest Hemingway, Tobias Wolf, and Chuck Palahniuk. Traditional education in writing can be a huge boost to your abilities, though there are some elements that we can take from these instructions that will be touched upon later, this is where you'll get years of practice in staccato sentence structure, dialogue that actually sounds like humans speaking, short story narrative creation, workshopping experience, and a skill with a red pen.

One of the biggest advantages to this track of work is the social element. You're going to meet your generation of writers, people who will become your colleagues and friends throughout your career. To this end, you'll also have a place to go if you ever need workshopping after college but prior to your use of an editor. It teaches you excellent critical skills and provides networking for later in life.

For those that are no creative writers, perhaps going for academic writing or journalism studies, this is also one of the best ways to establish connections. While the internet can very much instruct the non-fiction writer on ways to write to get the attention of a digital audience, you still need people you can go to, someone to read your work, someone who might know someone.

No matter what, the unfortunate truth of writing is that your prose can be amazing, but who you know is going to matter at getting someone else to notice.

Option 2: Secondhand Mentorship

This is like the first option, except without the years of crippling debt. It's also going to give you more freedom and be less strict in its teachings, which can help creative minds flourish. While I was in school (I went the padawan route) I nearly failed my very first writing class because it was solely based on writing technically correct sentences and I chaffed at the level of strictness.

So if you're afraid of Spartan instruction when it comes to writing, you might do better to find yourself some informal ways of gaining mentorship. This includes local writing groups, a personal mentor, and maybe even a class or two at the library.

There's plenty of resources for this, no matter where you're located in the world. And the great part about it is you get the social workshopping part without the thinly veiled competition and snobbery that can come from the college courses in writing. Not to mention, one on one help can be essential to writing well.

Option 3: Self-Made

You don't always need someone to hold your hand where writing is concerned. One of the most important things you're going to learn in any writing class is how to read other writer's work and how to take on the elements that work for you. If you're an avid reader (and if you're a writer then you are) then you're going to know how to do this, it's going to be a natural reaction for you.

The only way you become is a writer is by writing. So, if you want to skip some steps and cut out the distracting reads of work that's A-Okay. If you've got a story or a paper or an article burning inside you that needs to be written, then write it. Just go and don't let anyone tell you that you need to slow down or do anything else. If the inspiration and drive strikes you, then this is the path that's going to tell you to chase it.

Besides, if you find yourself desiring more instruction you can always get more later in life. The important thing is to reward and chase your own energy while you can.

Go Your Own Way

As Fleetwood Mac said, you can go your own way. You can choose one of these paths because they stand out to you as the one for you, or you can combine them in some way. Or maybe there's a secret third path that I've completely missed but you know all about. No matter what it is, go for it in the way that works for you and don't let anyone tell you that they have the secret to writing. Because they don't.

CHAPTER 3: THE BLANK PAGE

So, you've decided that you're a writer. You've taken the test and determined that you match Mr. Wendig's many-fold definition of writerly habits. Then you got the instruction you needed, in the way you wanted it. You've begun learning and begun writing and now you're ready to actually turn a bunch of words into sentences and sentences into paragraphs and those paragraphs into whole pages. You can see your finished book, the title of your article or blog post. You see your name in lights as the world rejoices at your insights and how smart you are.

But that's all in your mind's eye. Because right now your real eyes are staring at a blank page. It might be in a Word document on your computer or the top of a piece of notebook paper with a pen quaking in your hand. No matter the medium, a blank page is a blank page and it's scary.

One thing to know right off the bat: you're never going to escape the blank page. You could write three Pulitzer-winning books or full magazine exposes or academic papers about how you discovered intelligent life on Mars and you'll always be going back to a blank page when you're done. It's the nature of any creative craft. Doing one or two or twenty amazing things doesn't guarantee the next project. It's all going to be on you to get your next page filled with words.

But that's easier said than done, especially when that blank page is staring at you, all bright and empty.

There are a few ways you could tackle that first step and some of them are dependent on what kind of writing you're hoping to do. But there's a commonality between all of them. You're starting at the beginning no matter what, that's not going to change.

Option 1: Tell Us What You're Going to Tell Us

It may feel a little bit like an exercise from your grade school days where you'd start your paragraph explaining exactly what you're going to be talking about. It's a little basic but there's a reason these basic instructions and exercises exist. You want to be able to return to your roots if you have to. And this is one such example of some first-grade writing coming out to help you when you need it most.

Some of the greatest books out there start with a very bland and straightforward statement about how the story is going to go. The Hobbit, one of the greatest works of fantasy ever created, starts with the very simple sentence: "In a hole in the ground there lived a hobbit." Boom. The story goes from there. It sounds like a third grader might have written that sentence but it begins the first book in an epic line of fantasy novels. Sometimes simple is the best route.

So, if your book is about a cop, don't be afraid to just say "This story is about a cop." The thing people often forget when writing is that words on the page are not a commitment. There is such thing as an eraser, a backspace button. The version you write the first time is not going to be the final one people see. Though reading a book could be intimidating, you have to remember that that book also started as a blank page and what you're looking at is years of work and drafts and help from other people like a team of editors and an agent with notes.

Nothing is perfect the first time. So, if you need to simply say "It was raining one day…" then say it. It could be the next iconic book opener and if it's not, you can always rework it until the day your book goes to print. Nothing is stopping you from tweaking things to your heart's content.

The same thing is going to go for any form of non-fiction writing too. You can say "My article is about cats." The same rules apply: change it as much as you want while you're working, or keep it and let the world marvel at your ability to simply and eloquently draw them in. In writing rules exist, grammar is a strict mistress, but where things like this are concerned, there is no time-honored way to begin anything because we're all doing it every day and reinventing how it's done.

Option 2: Begin at the End

It's sometimes a very fun way to open a book that you show the reader the last scene, the last page, and let them figure out how we all end up there. One of my personal favorite examples of this and one of the best ones out there is the opening lines to the great American novel *To Kill a Mockingbird* by Harper Lee: "When he was nearly thirteen, my brother Jem got his arm badly broken." And without giving too much away (though anyone who went through the American public school system will have read this novel) that's exactly what the story is about by the end.

There are less cryptic ways, as well, to start at the end and work your way back to the beginning. You could start with your narrator telling the story in retrospect. Where is she now? How did she get there?

When writing, you want to know where you're going to end up. You don't need to know the exact scene; you don't need to know the exact words you're going to end your story on or how you're going to close out that big article you have due. But you need to know who your murderer is before you start the story, you need to know the point you're making at the end of the paper, and so on. Starting anything without knowing the ending is asking for trouble and one of the number 1 ways you'll find yourself victimized by writer's block.

You need to know where you're driving, otherwise you're not going anywhere, are you? You're just making turns on every street, deciding haphazardly on what to do.

George RR Martin talks about the two types of writers: the gardener and the architect. The architect is the writer who knows everything, they can see the scaffolding, they can see the exact path they're going to take to get there. They can see everything about the story. The gardener is the author who has the seeds, the ideas, they know what they'd like to see but they prefer to sit and watch things grow. Both writers are fine, both options are fantastic, but no matter what you need to know where things end.

So if you don't know where to start, then start at the end and work your way back.

Option 3: In Medias Res

This is an old film school trick and is often a place where you'll find action movies or horror flicks start. The phrase is a Latin one that shows up in film classes a lot that basically means starting in the middle of the action. The first shot is a firefight, someone running from cops, an argument between two characters. This is the happy medium between starting at the end and starting right at the beginning if neither of those work for you.

This is a great attention grabber and can help those who have the story formed up to a certain point. Maybe you don't know exactly how the climactic scene is going to end, but you know how it starts, so you're going to write that. And then, like starting at the end, we work our way up to that moment, we figure out how we got here.

It's an excellent choice for genre specific work, though it could work for anything, it's a device most commonly used in thrillers and horror books. But, if it works for you then go for it, make it your own. If it helps you get words on a page and start your project, then go for it.

Other Tricks

There are other tricks out there you can use to get words to fill that blank white page. One such trick is using notecards. There are a couple different ways to do it, depending on what you're writing. One option is using them to create scenes and an outline. This trick works best for those working on screenplays but can be used just as well for novels or other forms of fiction (and versions of it could be used for non-fiction writing as well). Essentially the idea is you outline a scene, not a chapter, not an entire arc, just one scene. Mark where it goes in the story (Act 1, part 1, however you want to break things up).

Essentially one these notecards would go like this:

Act 1, Scene 3: Jack meets Jill
Jack meets Jill at the supermarket. They talk. Both leave the conversation on a friendly note.

Easy right? It doesn't need to have the entire scene mapped out nor does there need to be complete dialogue. You just need the point, the main action, and who's involved. As for the act and scene markers, they don't need to be exact. You're always going to be adding in new scenes or elongating what's there. It's more for organizational purposes than being exact about how things are going to go.

Banging out a few notecards like that helps you visualize the scenes you know you want. And you can use the gaps between scenes to explore the story. The whole story doesn't need to be spelled out in notecards, in fact, it's better to have some gaping holes between outlined scenes. It's better for an organic build of the story and the tying of elements.

But scene outlines aren't the only ways you can use notecards to get yourself writing and evolving the work. This is specific to fiction writing but variations of it can work for non-fiction work as well. Basically, you take the notecards and use them to take inventory of your scenes. You can do this by using the cards to outline the setting, the props nearby, anything your characters might interact with.

Another way to do this is to use the notecards to keep track of the "top" and "bottom" story. This means the difference between what's actually happening, the action within the story, and the effects underneath. The top story, in our Jack and Jill scenario, is that Jack and Jill meet. The bottom story is that a friendship is being formed from that interaction.

Get it?

This can be a great way to tackle writer's block by figuring out exactly what the heck is going on in a story and why things are happening. It's also a great way to analyze scenes you might already have written and made sure they have some real intent going on in them.

That's one of the big things to help the creative juices to continue flowing while dealing with a case of writer's block: analyze what you have, analyze what you have planned, and make sure everything fits in with that ultimate goal and ultimate ending you're working towards. You can do this at any time in the writing process to help make things easier on yourself or at least distract from the anxiety that comes with writer's block and stoppages in writing.

So figure out the best way to start the story: whether it's a blunt announcement of what the story is about or a more cryptic look at how the story is going to end. Then take some time to analyze where things are going and why.

I NEED YOUR HELP

I really want to thank you again for reading this book. Hopefully you have liked it so far and have been receiving value from it. Lots of effort was put into making sure that it provides as much content as possible to you and that I cover as much as I can.

If you've found this book helpful, then I'd like to ask you a favor. Would you be kind enough to leave a review for it on Amazon? It would be greatly appreciated!

CHAPTER 4: WRITING FLOW IN THE THICK OF IT

So you've got the story going. It's begun. Things have started. You've begun some real work on your story and you're past that blank page in front of you and the glaring white nothingness of the beginning. Congrats! You've got over the biggest hump, the hardest part. It might not seem that way, but the beginning is truly the hardest part of writing. Once you're over that hump, things will get easier. But that doesn't mean they're easy period.

You've still got your work cut out for you. Because, like relationships with people, there are a series of phases you're going to go through with your writing. Think of the opening pages, that terrible difficult hurdle of starting like the gut wrenching fear of actually walking up to your crush and simply asking them out. You've gotten the courage to ask for a phone number or ask to get some coffee sometime and the great part is they said yes. It might not have been easy, it might have been messy but you've started, you're there. You're on the date and the relationship is beginning.

Phase 1: The Honeymoon

You're going to be in a honeymoon phase at first. That's a fact of anything. Watching your ideas first get down on the page and watching them unfurl is going to be unreal. Your characters will start talking, your paragraphs will start making sense. It's going to go from an abstract idea in your head to a fully-fledged and fleshed out series of paragraphs and content and stories.

It's fun and incredible to watch. You'll be hitting word count milestones no problem, banging out hundreds of words because it seems to just be pouring out of you. Your energy is up, you're ready to tackle this. Maybe you'll finish it months before you expected to. Everything is going to be great.

Until everything is not great because the honeymoon phase never lasts. After the first couple chapters, maybe a week or so of writing regularly, you're going to start to burn out. You're going to start to get tired, you're going to get distracted. It's normal and it's okay. It doesn't mean you're suddenly not a writer or somehow bad at what you do.

There's a reason athletes have off seasons, after all. No matter how good you are at something or how much you love it, you're going to have periods where you need a break. While you shouldn't take off months at a time like an athlete, you are allowed a day or two to regroup.

That being said, one of the best opening habits you can give yourself is the promise to write every day, as much as you can. We'll get to specific goals in a second. But while you're still in that honeymoon phase or before you start, promise yourself you're going to write every day, even if it's just one word a day on those nights when you're ready to pass out from exhaustion. Getting into that habit is going to save your butt later down the road, trust me.

So enjoy this honeymoon phase and get as much out of it as you can because it won't last but while you're in it, it's going to be an amazing time of creativity and energy for you. Get as much out of it as you can and recognize when it's starting to dwindle and accept that that is okay. It's a natural part of the process and all it means is that you're advancing, you're evolving to the next stage in your writing evolution.

Stage 2: Exhaustion and Self-Loathing

Not a very encouraging title is it? And hopefully, you don't find yourself in an actual relationship with someone that makes you feel this way. But this is also going to be a normal part of the writing process while working on a project. That exhaustion is going to set in and it's going to feel like you completely used up all your energy on some great first chapters but now you're out of juice and out of ideas.

Spoiler alert: you're not. You're just human.

As cliché as it sounds, the first step in dealing with this is accepting that it happens, that this is part of the process. You're going from the green, doe-eyed newbie to the jaded writer in the thick of writing something great. Acknowledge the exhaustion, but don't let it rule you. You don't need to play by the rules of your own fatigue.

This doesn't mean guzzle coffee and force things (though many writers do) but it means, rather, begin to recognize what your peak writing times are. For Ernest Hemingway, he would write before he even had breakfast, banging out two hours of writing each morning and then being done for the day. For others, they're night owls who can't work on any project if it's earlier than 10 pm. You can try out both and see what works for you. It's a great way to cheat the exhaustion system by avoiding periods when your exhaustion is going to feel the worst. Find the times in the day that works for you and book them out. Exhaustion can have other times.

That leaves the self-loathing thing. The fact of the matter is; no one likes the things they write. Even published books that are at their 10-year collector's editions are going to be disliked by the authors who cringe at their past work and think they can do better. Remember that first short story you wrote in high school? That first article you handed in as a newbie writer on the school newspaper? I imagine you don't like them very much. You're going to always feel that way, even about sentences you write two days ago.

You're always getting better, so past versions of yourself are going to look obsolete to you. That's okay, but remember that voice in your head isn't truth. It's just one person's opinion.

Are there neat tricks to get around your own self-doubt? Unfortunately, not really. The only thing you can really do is convince yourself to keep going. It won't be easy at first, but the only way to work through moments of self-doubt is to just power through and remember that drafts are drafts, you can always erase things and start over again, rearrange sentences, you name it.

But, when you find yourself trapped in the middle of a project with nowhere to go, there are some writing exercises you can do to try and get things flowing again.

Exercise 1: Conversations with Dead People

So, these people aren't actually dead. It was just a neat title (that may or may not be stolen from a *Buffy the Vampire Slayer* episode). But the point is this is an exercise all about getting to know your characters. Sometimes writing comes to a halt because you don't know what's supposed to come next, what anyone is supposed to say or do. Not knowing enough about your characters can really bog down your process sometimes.

So, one way to alleviate this is to set up a conversation with them, an interview of sorts. You, as the author, just begin by asking the character a question, any question you want or can think of. Then you let their answer (or maybe they avoid answering) guide the conversation from there on out. It can be an important question like asking them why they killed character B or it can be mundane, like asking them what they had for dinner. Either way, you'll get a conversation going.

Exercise 2: Creature Comforts

One great way to get a character to tell you more about themselves is to have them describe their home, more specifically their bedroom (if they have one) to you. It also helps to then have other characters describe that same space to you. You might find that the long descriptions end up in the story but if not you have a background on this person you did not have before. While character creation worksheets can be helpful for some, a more organic approach is sometimes the way people best get at who their characters are.

This exercise works for anywhere: a kitchen, an office, a dorm room, a balcony. Anywhere that your character frequents, you can have them describe to you. You'll be amazed at what you find out about your character after letting them talk to you for a while about the places they live.

Exercise 3: Writing Sprints

This is a nifty little trick I'm borrowing from the cult favorite TV writer Jane Espenson (*Buffy the Vampire Slayer, Game of Thrones, Once*

Upon a Time). She often has these writing sprints live on her Twitter. She encourages that you use them for any project you need to finish though, as a writer herself, she promotes them mainly as a tool for writers to get words on the page.

This is an exercise that's less about world building or character creation and a lot more about getting your word counts up to snuff. These usually last an hour, though shorter ones lasting 30 minutes exist as do longer ones lasting 2 hours. But the point is all the same: work and don't stop until time is called.

Writer's block can manifest as a distractive force: checking your phone, checking Facebook or email, googling random things on the internet, texting a friend, etc. You know what your sins are where procrastinating is concerned and this is designed to completely cut that out of the process. During writing sprints, you do nothing but write and work, whether you're writing the next chapter or planning or researching, for the allotted time. You turn off your phone, cut off your Internet connection, close all your distracting books. You make yourself a hermit to your writing for one hour and work on it.

It takes discipline but it's only a brief hour out of the day. If it's productive enough, maybe you hit your word count for the day and you're done. Maybe it encourages you to keep going for more and more. There's really only help and good things that can come from these writing sprints. And if you don't like the idea of doing them alone, you can get your friends involved or participate in one of Jane Espenson's many writing sprints on Twitter.

Stage 3: Don't Fear the Reaper

Coming to the end of a project can be both completely liberating and incredibly terrifying. As a result, you can have mind games with yourself over what to do and that results in some serious stalling of writing flow. You can be sabotaging yourself because you don't want it to end, or you're scared of what the ending could mean. Don't be.

If you've done your homework and the preplanning that you're supposed to do, then the end that's in sight won't be a surprise to you. You've prepared yourself for getting here the entire time with all the writing you've been doing and you don't need to stop now, though a voice in your head may be trying to convince you to do just that.

Coming to the end of things is harder than you think. When you start the work, you may be completely gunning for the end. It's everything you've been working towards. You earned it. But when it's a few chapters or hundred words in sight, you'll likely have one of two reactions:

End too quickly
Let it drag on

Both are equally problematic issues that can arise from coming to the end of a work and not knowing what to do about it. Ending to fast seems to be the more common of the two, with people likely just stopping in the middle of the action or finding ways to wrap something up too neatly. Maybe you cut that last scene you intended or maybe you completely left out that final argument you had for your article. You just want it done. It doesn't make you a bad person, or a bad writer. It happens to everyone. The trick is recognizing it and going back and fixing it. If you need things to end to be done and have a break, that's okay. Just know that, in the next draft, you'll be doing some elongating work on that section.

Then there is the other option of not knowing when to quit because maybe you just can't bring yourself to say it's over. For that one as well you'll just have to let it run its course, write what you want and then, at the end of it all, go back during the editing process and chop it down. It can be a gut wrenching process to take things out, but it's a very necessary one for you to get things accomplished and complete. And you'll learn quite a bit about editing after all is said and done.

CHAPTER 5: IT'S DONE, NOW WHAT

You have written your last word, completed the last page. You've put a period at the end and called it quits on the project. It's finished, it's written, you have a round of applause for yourself and maybe grab a few drinks.

But you're not done.

You can give yourself a break. You can take some time off. In fact, it's best to get yourself away from a project for a while after you've completed it. If you're someone who participates in NaNoWriMo then you know that after you complete the work at the end of November, you take December and January off and don't return to edit it until February. You might not want to wait so long, or maybe you do. It's up to you really, but the point is that you'll want to take some time off and it's good for you to do so.

But when you return to a work, you need to be ready to take it on completely, red pen and all. This part is going to be difficult because, as the writer, everything in the work is going to seem vital and important to you. Cutting things doesn't mean they were bad or poorly formed (though that can be a reason you cut something). All it means is that it was not necessary. Writing is about simplicity and a lot of people forget that.

It doesn't really seem like simplicity is the spice of life when looking at something like Shakespeare or JRR Tolkien, but the fact of the matter is saying what you mean in three words is a lot better than a whole flowing paragraph of flowery language. That's why you should abide by this simple rule when taking a red pen to your work:

Edit as if you're getting paid a dollar for every word you remove.

You want excessive adjectives gone. You want dialogue tags only around when they need to identify a speaker once or a conversation, bare minimum. It'll hurt your soul to remove some sections and maybe even to remove entire chapters or characters who just didn't quite fit into the world you were creating, but it's a necessary evil of the process.

That being said, editing drafts can be an incredibly daunting task and one you don't want to undertake lightly. Underestimating the editing process can lead to some serious frustration and a lot of stalling because it's just so much more than you expected or wanted out of the process. But knowing what you're getting yourself into before you begin is crucial to being prepared for what's coming down the road.

So the first step is to take things in chunks. You can say you're going to edit one chapter a day, or a half chapter. But that also doesn't mean you should beat yourself up over spending longer times that normal on sections. Maybe it takes a whole two days to get a conversation in one chapter just the way you want it and that's okay too. Unlike your word count, this isn't as strict of a scheduled regimen and you'll need to allow time for yourself to think about things out.

It's not unlike a puzzle you need to solve. You'll need to test out different pieces in different places, omitting things, adding things, playing with word choice. It's not an exact science and you'll want to be as thorough as possible. But, again, nothing is set in stone until he day it goes to print. You can always go back and fix an edit you don't like, add something back in, take it away again, you name it. Don't feel married to the first change you make or even the fifth. You can always change things.

Use outlines as edit guides

While you may be using outlines at the beginning to get the narrative arc down (and you should be), they can also be used during the editing process to as a way to look at everything in reverse. You can plug parts of the story and steps in a character narrative into existing outlines to help make sense of the story, see what works, see what doesn't work, and see how you can best sculpt the story.

- **The Monomyth:** This is one of the oldest, in fact, possible the oldest, story cycles in the world. This is a storytelling outline that has been traced out by Joseph Campbell, outlined in his book *Hero With a Thousand Faces*, that stretches all the way back to Babylon. The idea is that we're all writing the same story over and over again, the same parts, the same plot twists, the same characters, all based on the root story *The Epic of Gilgamesh* from Mesopotamia. You can do some further research on the story cycle yourself since there's plenty of variations, but the basic tenants are the blocks that build every great story you've ever seen from *Star Wars* to Disney animated features.

- **Dan Harmon's Story Circle:** This might technically be a variation on the monomyth since Harmon did use that as his starting point for this, but it's an entire character based outlining method that works great for non-genre specific literary fiction (or genre writing that wants to be more character focused, like a Stephen King horror novel). This is another one you can look up and make your own but the basic breakdown of this outline is that a character wants something, they get it, and consequences ensue. As all great Broadway musicals have an "I Want" song, all great stories need to start with someone who wants something they don't have, whether they're hero or villain or should want the thing in the first place.

- **The Traditional Triangle:** This one is the story structure we all know and have been taught since grade school. This is the starting point that leads to the rising action, the climax, then the falling action. It's almost entirely plot based and great for genre fiction writing help. If you want to make sure your plot works, plug in the points in this outline and check to see if everything checks out correctly.

- **Nonfiction Options:** For those of you working on articles, papers, blog posts, or anything else that's not the next great American novel, there's plenty of ways you can use outlines to help your work too. Essentially you'll want to make sure you have at least three body elements to support whatever your topic and/or thesis is. You can have more, but you don't want less, so keep that in mind while editing your work.

Editing can be a rough and painful process, but the thing to remember is that you've done the hard part. You've created something out of nothing. You took that first blank page you were staring at and turned it into an entire paper or article or book or screenplay. Editing is just making sure the polish looks good, the paint coats are drying, and everything fits in neatly where it should be.

Editing is your chance to make a nicely polished and squeaky clean version, that thing you've been thinking about in your head for so long now that's finally a reality. Don't skimp on it and don't let it get you down too much. It can be tough, but nothing is tougher than writing from scratch. So if you made it this far you've done great, you've beat that writer's block, you've gotten something accomplished. Pat yourself on the back and poor that class of wine.

CHAPTER 6: GOOD HABITS TO REMEMBER

Interspersed with all the information above, is a few great habits you can insert into any point in your writing process to make sure things are done to the best of your abilities and showing off the best work you have inside you. These things aren't for everybody and they might work better in different situations than what people are used to, but they're not bad ways to start off and not bad things to get into.

Take these with both a grain of salt and some serious consideration because some might seem strange but they can really help you in the long run.

Meditation

This is an example of one that's not for everyone, but something that's a great and solid option for calming the brain. I didn't start practicing meditation as it pertained to writing until my senior year of undergraduate. I had a professor who ended every class with a meditation session she leads where she had us think about the work we did, the work we still wanted to do and basically had us wind down for the last twenty minutes after two hours of workshopping.

You don't have to do it exactly this way. You can do it before you start writing to help clear your head of distractions and make sure you have a focus. You can do it at the beginning of your day as a way to calm yourself and avoid stress later. You can do it at the end of the day as a way to wind down from everything. You can do it sitting down, standing up, laying on your back, right before you go to bed, whatever it is you want, you have the option. Meditation is about your brain, your soul, what makes you tick and what helps you relax. Or you don't have to do it at all, your choice.

Condition Yourself with Environment

By this I mean, you want to create an environment where you're conditioned to expect yourself to write. You can write wherever you want, on an airplane, during your subway commute, in a coffee shop, on a park bench, wherever it strikes you. But, it doesn't hurt to create an environment and situation where you expect to write. For a lot of writers, this means a time of day or maybe specific clothes. I had a professor who could only write if she was wearing pajamas so she often left her pajamas on during the day to give herself an environment to write in.

It was mentioned earlier in this book that you can pick specific times of day to write and that falls into this option as well. You may find waking yourself up at the crack of dawn to write Hemingway style is what gets the best juices flowing or you may find that you can't think a single creative thought until after 10 pm and a cup of tea. It doesn't matter, as long as it's consistent. Consistency is going to, obviously, be what keeps you going in your work. If you do the same thing, constantly, you'll be trained to do it. There's a saying that you make habits until, one day, you've found that your habits make you. This is one such example.

Set a Goal and Stick to It

Writers always say you should be writing every day. And it's true, you should be writing every day, but sometimes it's also just no possible to get down entire chapters or pages in one day when you work full time or are perhaps a student. Stephen King will tell you that anyone who wants to be a writer needs to devote themselves to getting at least 2,000 words written a day. For the seasoned author, and someone like King who can afford to make writing his full-time job, that's not too tricky. But for students and parents and working professionals, that's a tall order sometimes.

And you shouldn't feel bad about not living up to certain

standards. The best way to avoid letting yourself down is to set achievable, but challenging goals. Some days you're only going to be able to get a word or a sentence down. Those days will happen, don't beat yourself up over it. The point is that you're making an effort to write. But on days when you do have time and should be writing, set yourself a goal of words to achieve. Maybe 2,000 is the number that works for you, maybe your ambition and can manage 3,000, maybe you just want 500. Test your limits, test what you can do, and make it work for you. It's always better to have a low goal and hit it than something completely out of your range.

So make yourself a goal you can reach, and something you know that you can hit without things getting a little too stressful for you. We can't all write full time, but we do have the option of writing every day so chase that option.

Limit Distractions

This is something every writer can and should be doing constantly. You don't need to completely lock yourself way like a writing spring style session for every time you sit down to write, but you do need to make sure that you're getting down on a number of things that could distract you from getting writing down. In the age of the internet and computers with word processing capabilities, it can be very hard to take away virtually all the distractions that could come your way. But, there are handy tricks.

The best thing to do is turn of your WiFi on your computer while you're working. Or simply take your laptop to some place where you can access the WiFi. Either way, you're cutting yourself off from the internet for a bit to avoid the temptation of opening a tab to Google something because you suddenly needed to know exactly where mozzarella cheese comes from and how it's made. Those weird things pop up in your brain and they can take over your thoughts and your time if you let yourself chase them. So don't. Cut yourself off from the internet for a bit like your parents and grandparents once lived their lives. You'll survive, trust me.

The other big thing you'll want to do is stow that phone. Smartphones are nifty gadgets to keep you occupied on commutes or long flights but they can be a productivity-destroying distraction when you let them be. So turn it off if you're going to have it near you. Emergencies happen so set up a way someone can get a hold of you if they need to and don't let the phone tempt you. You can also set it off to the side to charge while you work so you won't be tempted to reach out and check it every time you pause in writing.

Another great way to limit distractions is to get a mood background that suits you. Get a tower fan to generate white noise, work in a crowded park with non-rhythmic background sounds, or completely cancel everything with noise canceling headphones. I had friends who can only write while a TV or radio of some sort is playing in the background and some friends who need total peace and quiet to get writing done. So, whatever works for you figure it out and stick to it.

Choose a Music

This is linked to the background music bit with a bit more specifics because all writers, inevitably, will talk about the best music for them to write to. It's not unlike a painter sticking earbuds in their ears for the entire time they put brush to canvas. You need something that puts you in the right mood for what you're doing. Music can really be that for a writer and, sometimes, it can even completely crush your writer's block if you pick the right tunes.

8tracks offers plenty of user generated, as well as staff generated, soundtracks for writing in virtually any genre you can think of. If instrumental music is more your speed, you can also write to the sounds of film scores or traditional classic music. The fact of the matter is;s the music you choose can make or break your ability to create a work. You might be stuck on a scene and then hear the epic, sweeping score of *Lord of the Rings* and suddenly you have the inspiration and drive to keep going. Music can do that for you while you're writing, so don't be afraid to use it.

There's plenty of more tricks out there and little things you're going to discover along the way that can make your writing flow better and help you be the best you can be at writing. But remember, habits and tricks aren't going to be the magic ticket. It's always going to start with you, your wants, your ideas, your ability to sit and write, your discipline, so always remember that before putting all your faith in a writing playlist or a comfy pair of sweatpants to write in.

Everything you need is already inside you, you just need the courage and the right tools to unlock that potential and set it free. That's what habits are all about. They can make you, once you devote yourself to them.

CONCLUSION

So, what have we learned? Writing is hard work. There's no getting around that. Many people want to ask established writers if they have advice for young writers because they want some kind of quick fix, an easy out. They want something that makes the entire process go by a lot easier and quicker. The fact of the matter is, it doesn't go quick and it won't just because you want it to.

Writing is a lot of discipline and hard work. It's a muscle you constantly have to flex to make sure it stays sharp and in tune. The only way you're going to succeed is through work. Some people get lucky, but luck itself is only going to take you so far. You need to want it and that means you need to be willing to discipline yourself, change your habits, and sculpt your mind into making your writing flow steady and worth it.

As for where you can find yourself some further reading and further resources here's a list of things to check out to help overcome that writer's block and keep yourself writing:

- **642 Things to Write About**: A series of books filled with writing prompts (some themed, some not) as put forward by the San Francisco Writer's Grotto. It's got daily prompts, unique prompts, fiction prompts, journal entry prompts, and virtually everything in between.

- **Letters to a Young Poet by Rainer Maria Rilke**: This book is a famous classic work at this point. It's a series of letters written by Rilke to a young Franz Xavier Kappus while he worked at poetry during his military service. It's been a staple guide to artists everywhere about how you should approach the creation of art and not give up on your dreams

- **Hero with a Thousand Faces by Joseph Campbell**: The book mentioned in previous chapters that details how we're all writing one story with different environments and characters. It's a great outline to use for your writing and a great way get things started when you need it.

- **Dan Harmon's Story Circle**: Easily accessible on his blog, this diagraph outlines how to write character-centric versions of the monomyth.

There's plenty more out there. There's an entire world waiting to read your work. You need only believe in yourself enough to devote your time to it and you'll be amazed at what you can accomplish.

So, writers, far and wide, old and young, you've got the power in you already, you've got the skills and you've got the brains. Like I said at the beginning of this book, you need only to step out of your own way, beat down the voices in your head telling you that you're not good enough or not smart enough or you'll never be as good as your favorite author. Find ways to erase the noise from your mind, especially your own voice, and get down to what really matters: the writing itself.

I hope this work has been a help to at least one person out there who struggled with their writing. You're heard and you're certainly not alone in the struggle. Keep writing kid and you'll go very, very far.

LIKE THIS BOOK?

Check us out online or follow us on social media for exclusive deals and news on new releases!

 https://www.pinnaclepublish.com

 https://www.facebook.com/PinnaclePublishers/

 https://twitter.com/PinnaclePub

 https://www.instagram.com/pinnaclepublishers/

Printed in Germany
by Amazon Distribution
GmbH, Leipzig